Distant
Music

Distant Music

Poems by

Joan Annsfire

HEADMISTRESS PRESS

Copyright © 2014 by Joan Annsfire
All rights reserved.

ISBN-13: 978-0692316092
ISBN-10: 0692316094

This book may not be reproduced, in whole or in part, including illustrations, in any form (beyond that permitted by Sections 107 and 108 of the U.S. Copyright Law and except by reviewers for the public press), without written permission from the publishers.

Cover Art: Robert Giard photograph of George Segal's Gay Liberation Monument, Sheridan Square, NYC (1980). Copyright © Estate of Robert Giard. Photograph courtesy of the Stephen Bulger Gallery and Yale Collection of American Literature, Beinecke Rare Book and Manuscript Library.

Cover & book design by Mary Meriam

PUBLISHER
Headmistress Press
60 Shipview Lane
Sequim, WA 98382
Telephone: 917-428-8312
Email: headmistresspress@gmail.com
Website: headmistresspress.blogspot.com

Contents

Distant Music

Life was a party I crashed clumsily,
a voyeur, a wallflower,
standing on the sidelines of weddings, births,
nearly everything that binds the social fabric.

A shy stranger in a room
full of other people's friends,
my little plate of gender rolls
dipped in the bitter sauce of obligation;
small, wilted canapés on a tarnished platter.

I arrived with little more than my youth,
fleeing my shabby kitchen
that came alive at night,
its counters and floors awash in roaches;
it was there I prepared dinner
and plotted revolution.

Pesky relatives claimed a husband
could pull me out of squalor
but, to me, their stories were but cautionary tales,
peppered with maybes and should-have-beens.

They swore I would rue the day
I walked out of their party
yet, I still savor the moment I opened
that fated door.

Beyond it lay an outcast's world;
mountains of treasure scattered
in bright and jumbled piles,
a veritable carnival of disorder.

I heard a circus-song of odd harmonies
a merry-go-round of alternatives,
striking every chord in my imagination,
resounding, vibrating, seducing
with wild and discordant song.
As I listened every hair rose up
and stood at attention.

Moments later,
I found myself dancing.

Currents

We were in love and almost young
that summer we braved the Rogue River together,
tumbling down and over the
rapids in an inflatable kayak
buoyant as the bouncing craft on churning water.

Drifting farther and farther from view,
we floundered, teetering on the intangible boundary
between daring and stupidity,
the green banks and big sky wove
a magnificent, emerald tunnel
disguising the overpowering currents,
sweeping us toward the sea.

The Rogue was low and rowdy that year,
not easily manipulated by amateurs,
finally we gave in to reason
and boarded the large raft
to allow more practiced arms to raise oars
and challenge the treacherous waters.

If will alone could replace skill
we would have conquered that river;
gone down laughing and twisting
around jagged rocks,
joyriding on the rushing rapids.

Or perhaps,
if we'd dropped anchor in the furious current
winter would have never come
and we could have remained midstream,
balanced on that far edge of youth
forever.

Covering Ground

From inn to train station,
the days rolled over the rails:
Copenhagen, Innsbruck, Barcelona,
names bleeding together as, at each stop,
we lifted our packs to begin again.

Strangers in train compartments
offered us bread, cheese, snippets of their lives
and we listened ravenously
because we were young, our baggage light,
the tracks enticingly infinite,
we moved with quick certainty
and vowed to stay as long as our money lasted.

A map in my pocket, a stash in your shoe,
the months unwound and there was always
another cathedral, another fountain.
We had reasons, plentiful as unlived years,
to love a life without borders.

Winter brought cold nights in seedy hotels
without heat or hot water
where plumbing shrieked and visitors
came and went at all hours
as if pulled by strange, internal tides.

We used our room bidets as urinals
and learned to ask for extra blankets
in several languages.

Road weariness crept in slowly
like the damp of British parlors where we took tea;
perpetual observation made us feel
more like voyeurs than participants
in our own lives.

Back on familiar soil, we went our separate ways;
I opted for California,
you retreated to the Midwest.
Later, I heard that, once home,
you never dared step
aboard a plane again.

But, I continued to scour the earth
searching to regain that elusive prize
we claimed so casually in our wanderings;
the intense, immeasurable hunger
that was somehow lost
in transit.

Across the Table

The hours,
we sat in a cafe, in the sun
writing treatises, discussing
changes in the wording, changes in the air,
the electric energy of ideas,
a huge banner unfurling into the
boundless space
of our vision.

I remember,
the distinctive rhythm of your voice,
your powerful current of energy,
the understated music
of your quiet listening.

Later,
I replayed such simple motions:
your pen tapping against the table,
your fingers moving around the rim of a glass,
I imagined touching your shoulder
but being less than brave
my actions did not flow as easily
as the words that took shape
on blank paper.

Now,
it seems strange
to have kept a special place
for time passed so uneventfully,
a day like any other,
full of opportunities
lost or squandered.

Looking back,
I marvel
that the world did not pause
and hold its breath
in those years when life was fast and dense
and as close as I have come
to flying.

Under Siege

How we battled on
that first year; big-city girls away from home,
we dodged salt pellets, knee-knockers
and clouds of pepper gas
and, as the tanks rolled down High Street,
we were high on freedom,
had held our own in meaner streets,
challenged but undaunted.
Behind the lines of bayonets,
we were currents, strong and wild;
charged by the electricity of danger,
their weapons couldn't hold us back
from a world changing faster
than we ever believed
possible.

How we came home
to the funky apartment with
the rickety, old porch swing,
our stodgy roommates,
too timid or cautious
to try their hands at revolution,
busy playing other games
like seduce the professor, become a great artist
or just lay as low as possible
until the strike closed the university
leaving us only
the school of the streets.

How we got stoned
on grass, hash and acid;
once, tripping together,
I saw eagles with huge talons
trying to take you from me,

but I didn't need birds of prey
because you disappeared anyway,
to the house of your latest boyfriend
as I, your abandoned comrade-in-arms,
stumbled through my acid-induced haze
alone.

How I holed up
in my room as the cold crept in
from every leaky window pane,
reliving the days of love and war,
remembering the way your pointed teeth
punctuated your sly smile,
the casual toss of your head,
and later, the silences
that grew as long as the shadows
of late autumn unfolding.

How I cried
in the snow that winter
when the inevitable
rotation of the earth
was the only revolution in sight,
my hopes folded
and were carried away
like the tents of nomads moving on
to more promising territory.

How I was laid low,
under the weight of tradition,
heavier than the force of gravity;
transporting you to a place
far beyond my reach;
platitudes carved in stone
came down from every mountaintop,
laying waste to my furtive dreams
and eviscerating my fragile universe
of delicate and bright desire.

Deserted Beaches

I came to the edge of the ocean
barren and brittle as the
blackened branches of trees after fire;
a message transformed into charcoal,
a carving of scar tissue upon the land.

Your illness, your death
hardened me to a cinder,
I walked the beach a skeleton,
a grain of sand against the sky.

I remember the small things;
your hands selecting peaches,
moving slowly over the rows of ripe fruit,
your hairless head bound in Balinese fabric
that, like your life, had begun to unravel.

I came to the edge of the ocean
to spread small remembrances of you on the sand,
like ashes flung over the side of a boat,
and the futile words tossed after;
these lives, not nearly time enough
to make up for those long, hard years
of preparation.

I came to the edge of the ocean
to listen to secrets waves pass on to the shore,
to learn why you came to live among us
and why you left so soon.

Like a hungry bird
seeking seed amid the seaweed,
I search for sustenance
in wide and empty spaces.

Strange November

Turquoise water like blown glass rises,
smooth sheets lift and fall like breathing,
a sailboat passes under the Golden Gate Bridge
wrapped in the unseasonably, hot smog
of a winter that refuses to come.

The two-towered bridge stands,
filtered through a thick curtain of warm air and silence,
transformed, now that Diana has joined
the circus of souls congregated
where the land is parted by water and salt.

They say she took a taxi to the bridge,
left her wallet on the railing
so the newspapers would know
how to spell her name.

Some heard her scream and curse invisible demons,
taunting disembodied voices that begged her to jump,
until she flung herself into air,
escaping a world reverberating
with confusion and inner noise.

I knew her seventeen years ago,
just moments beyond the tight circle of childhood;
we were both lost, bitter and afraid;
spit out into a world too mean to swallow.

We claimed to know that, in this life,
anything could happen,
but then were surprised and dismayed
when it did.

Yesterday, I sat with her friends on the museum lawn,
trying to make sense of the unfathomable,
to remember Diana and celebrate her life
as well as our own dogged, persistent survival.

A gull flew overhead calling out
its loud, demanding message,
so like Diana to return in feathers
and mock those of us
who have chosen to remain
a while longer.

Back here, on the translucent bay,
the one lone sailboat has taken down its sail
and now requires a motor
to steer it back to shore,
otherwise, it would bob forever
on a windless surface of green glass
lacking the simple power to reverse direction
and return home.

Legacy

I.
At forty, the mirror reflects
my mother's face, her last face,
frozen in time at forty-eight,
before the sunken cheeks, hollow eyes,
and yellow skin stretched tight
beneath my pink hand.

She is trying to speak
from her hospital bed,
words filtered through clenched teeth,
as if her jaws were wired shut.
She says everything tastes metallic now,
from the poison they call
chemotherapy.

I am her twenty-two year old daughter
but nothing in my brief span of years
has prepared me for this grief we share
in separate sorrow.

I am young
but believe myself to be wise,
I am afraid
but keep pretending to be brave;
they need me now
my father, my sister, my grandmother
we are going to the hospital
and, for some reason, I am driving.

I hold the steering wheel tightly
so they can't see
how my hands are shaking.

We are still at the stage
of making meaningless,
reassuring noises,
words that none of us believe
any longer.

Although the cancer
has overtaken her body
she returns home
and, from time to time, emerges
from behind the dense,
heavy curtain of her pain
to do routine, unremarkable things,
transformed into small miracles.

We walk through the neighborhood
on an Ohio afternoon in early May;
the air is heavy with the scent of hyacinth and lilac,
the ordinary, tree-lined street
vibrates with light and color
as, for an instant, I see it through her eyes,
one last look at the lush, green season
when so much new life begins.

Now we talk freely of the past,
her childhood, the early days of her marriage,
the ordeal of giving birth
to me, to my sister.
She speaks of a third pregnancy
ending in abortion
because there wasn't time
or money enough for another child.

This rush of words becomes the bridge
between her life and mine;
time contracts and collapses
narrowing the space between us.

Small and afraid,
she is still my mother,
but no longer the parent in control;
I am her child, her witness,
the bearer of her history,
although the fact of her dying
still remains unspoken.

When she returns to the hospital
we are all aware that it is
for the last time;
she reaches out and strokes my hair,
touches my face for the first time
since childhood,
says that her main regret
is that she will never see
her children grow up.

And somewhere, in the unlit spaces of my soul,
my grief is cleansed with relief, knowing that
I will no longer live
in the shadow
of her expectations.

On mother's day I give her a poem,
she reads it, cries,
says that the person
who was my mother
has already departed
and only a shell of disease
remains.

She is being held captive
in a disfigured, bloated body,
connected to life only
by chemicals and pain,
the skin covering her face is so thin

I can see the shape of the skull beneath;
she looks at me with glazed eyes,
windows through which
her life is escaping.

At home that evening
I count out sleeping pills;
blue for sodium amytal,
yellow for nembutal,
and arrange them in piles of ten;
her pills, the last remnants,
of a lifetime
of sleepless nights.

My father is the one who
helps her take them.
Using a pin, he pricks both ends of each capsule,
and, after she swallows them all,
he climbs into her narrow hospital bed
and holds her until the pain is gone.

II.
Now, eighteen years later
with all I inherited from my mother
came her genes for manufacturing
these flawed cells in my own body.

My diagnosis is read to me like
the verdict in a bad courtroom drama,
lab reports are passed from hand to hand
while doctors throw out phrases
like "forty-percent survival rate"
referring to my life as though they were
discussing a game of golf.

But the only thing I see
is my mother's ravaged face,

wiry hair, narrow lips, almond-shaped eyes.
In my mirror our two faces merge,
form one death's head;
her legacy,
my inheritance.

Yesterday, I was flesh and blood and bone,
I experienced the earth
only through my hands,
my eyes, the soles of my feet.
Today all the rules and boundaries have changed,
my own body has turned against me
and I feel its betrayal on the deepest level.
I stand naked, skeletal,
pared down to the root and bleeding.

I dream that I am running
through a burning house
and each board I step on is in flames
and gives way beneath my feet.
I keep running even though
there is no beam that can support my weight
and fire is everywhere.

I sort through my life
like a fire survivor sifting through ashes,
finding little of meaning or value left
among the ruins.

So now, one by one,
I begin to untangle
the complex web of strands
that bind me to this life.
I breathe deeply
and, for a moment, the panic subsides.
I unclench my fists
and terror that, for decades,

has clamped down my shoulders
begins to fall away.

When I speak now,
I can say anything;
when I look, I can see everything.
Words keep springing up like fresh new grass
and time has slowed to a crawl;
flashbacks of memory
reeling off like clips from old movies,
forty years in a breath, an instant,
a flicker of light.

My life has been reduced to two items
that consume the whole of my existence:
my lab reports and the tumor itself,
a fearsome entity,
suspended in solution;
a demon with a life
all its own.

These mysterious oracles
have been traveling
in the hands of my partner,
who is neither impressed,
nor intimidated
by western medicine;
who, after working in a hospital for years,
has a very high regard
for second and
third opinions.

Another doctor, a specialist,
has agreed to re-examine the evidence
to determine whether or not he concurs
with the vision of
the former medical prophet.

A reprieve is being handed down,
a voice on the phone
now assures me that
a mistake has been made,
says that after relatively minor surgery,
I will be able to return
to the world I barely remember
where the future stretches and yawns,
seductively infinite,
and full of possibility.

There is a pause,
a wait for wild, thunderous applause,
but I can offer only
simple acknowledgement
followed by silence
as one thin shaft of light
penetrates deep, still water.
Coming up from the ocean floor,
the task that remains
is one that must be undertaken slowly
and with great care.

III.
Today, back at work
the streets are drenched with
a steady, quiet rain.

It is four o'clock on a stormy afternoon
in mid-December.
I am sitting at the window
hypnotized by the sound of rain, the stillness,
not worrying about my journey home,
next weekend, or what I will eat for dinner.

It is the evening of the winter solstice,
and the sun
is already setting.

There is a strange and beautiful awakening
that comes with darkness:
cataclysmic, irreversible
as the first opening of a newborn's eye.

This is the gift of vision
unfolding before me tonight,
the longest night
of the year.

Damage

Everything you love will leave you.

That phrase repeated in my head,
to the rhythm of our footfalls
as we walked over the covered bridge,
the day smelled warm and green,
free from the confines of our van, weighed down
with the necessities and disjointed fragments
of our lives.

Her gaze was elsewhere,
gray and empty as the highway.
I stood, hypnotized by her overcast eyes
enveloping my universe,
swallowing up all light.

My passion was bloody and raw.

But I was a ghost, a shadow,
removed from polite society,
the inner terror that awaited me
was mine and mine alone.

Everything you love will leave you.

An endless mantra
that rattled around my head,
words of exile that dashed for
the ever-receding border
of my dreams.

My love could not do anything but damage.

I had seen images of her world
in every film, newspaper and magazine,
but the plays and stories like my own
foretold only of sad and sorry lives.

Our paths diverged that summer
hers swerved toward paved streets with lighted houses;
mine opened onto wide rocky cliffs
barren and bounded by wilderness.

When we said goodbye, we hugged like desperate strangers.

First Summer

That first summer after recovery,
the Oregon landscape,
was a work of art, vivid and deep;
slices of cloudless blue opened
into evergreen valleys
bounded by a massive,
all-encompassing
horizon.

We swam naked
in water clear, fast and cold,
dove and darted under electric sunshine,
yellow and pink limbs moving
strong and hard against the current,
high on the exhilaration of narrow escape
and second chances.

Still feeling fragile, uncertain.
the hollow place on my thigh etched
with a deep purple scar,
the mark of one who had shed her skin
then emerged, transformed
into an undeterrable rush
of water.

Round, flat leaves, half-lit by sunlight,
fluttered in the late afternoon breeze
and the western wind carried notes of a tune
drifting in from somewhere
far away.

Later that night in the cabin
other songs came to me;
shrill crickets called down the twilight
as August faded into September,
like the last beads added
to a long string of warm,
summer evenings.

Melody, melancholy, melodrama,
melanoma, melanoma,
how can a word so like music
imply an end to this fierce beauty?

Syllables whose sound alone conjures up
images of villas on the Mediterranean
and flamboyant Spanish dances.

Yet, all that summer,
that single word reverberated inside my head
until the leaves themselves whispered it
and it was tossed from rock to rock
by the river.

To say that you can only appreciate
being here instead of being at work,
yet refuse to imagine
being here compared to not being at all,
is to filter out
this incredible sensation
of intense, unstoppable joy.

Instead, take it within you:
marvel at the dance of light and shadow
on the water's moving surface,
rejoice in the masterpiece
of an unconquerable river
beneath a gradually
darkening
sky.

Descent

If I could,
I would have chosen other folks as family,
people who pounded grain, wove baskets,
gathered water and
sang down the moon.

Instead I came from those
devoured by history
and consumed by sadness,
whose memories, like Cossacks on horseback,
pursue them down blood-drenched,
nightmare streets.

Tormented by twisted visions
of attics, cattle cars
and shower room ceilings clawed
by desperate fingernails,
they bear witness to a knowledge
as insidious as light
filtered through a lampshade
of human skin.

I recall the rage in my mother's voice
as she tossed back another scotch,
my father's cutting humor,
his readiness to fight at the smallest slight,
the tallies they kept,
the wariness they carried.

My grandparent's closets
overflowed with food
as if to placate the relentless vigilantes
of hunger and fear,
just in case, they said, *just in case.*

Yes, my ancestors had few words for joy
but many to express sorrow,
I know that, even in death,
they do not lie in meditative silence
but gather in rowdy confrontation
shouting out their difficult
and angry love.

Release

I grew up fast. Not straight and tall,
but bent and fractured,
like the trajectory of light through water.
I embodied imperfection,
yet survived, so I know
my failings served me well.

I was born certain that I never wanted children,
but plagued by the realization
that it was a preference
my parents shared.

Memories of childhood return,
not as a joyous outpouring of love
but as searing pain, a white-hot flame
that fries flesh and melts bone.

These interludes happen
at the most inopportune moments.
At the gym a I overheard
a doting mother, comforting her child,
"What's wrong, my little honey bear?"
she asked in dulcet tones, and, as she spoke,
I felt my skin ripped from my body
leaving every nerve raw, exposed
and pulsating in bitter air.

Some things we are born to,
others are of our own design.
but neuroses are a scourge
passed down from parent to child
and, in my case, they fit me like a glove.

Before you leap, it is wise to take stock of the area
where you will fall,
but when it comes to family
you simply close your eyes and take your chances.

My mother was my biggest fan and my fiercest competitor.
Together we danced the women's dance
of ambivalence that sometimes passes for love.
The first time she ever touched my face with feeling
was when she was sure she was dying.

At twenty-two I became her successor,
the oldest female on my splintered family tree;
an ancient, yet unwrinkled woman,
whose entire life was behind her.

Youth was only one of the treasures lost
in those hard years when pretending became a lifestyle
and forgetting, an exalted art.

It was then I came to view death
much like orgasm, blissful release
followed by deep, dreamless sleep.

Sea Change

When I first saw the Pacific
it surpassed all my expectations;
jade green and ferocious,
it surged and sucked at massive rock
like a feral animal ripping into soft flesh,
grinding everything in its path to sand.

This primal stage of life's beginning
proved an antidote to despair,
a magnetic force so overwhelming that,
following my mother's death,
I left Ohio and drove west
until the land yielded to ocean
in a churning display
of power and solace
through motion.

I heard breaking questions crash
and gulls scream wild,
wind-lashed responses;
poignant and dissonant
as a ship horn's fading song.

I watched footprints and fish bones disappear
in wave after wave as the shore
was perpetually wiped clean;
I felt the salty, seaweed balm soothe
my formerly landlocked mind.

California beaches are full
of miracles and infinite wonder,
I still tread upon them lightly
as if walking on water.

There, birth and death merge, trade places,
as, with each powerful pull of the tide,
the world begins
anew.

In the Old Neighborhood

In the old neighborhood
the young dykes are impenetrably sealed
in black leather, have pierced lips and eyebrows,
piercing eyes,
cool laughter bounces off
their smooth, hard faces.

I wear myself more comfortably now,
my older body baggy, stretched and
soft as a favorite pair of flannel pajamas;
I have slipped into that category
populated by mothers and grandmothers
who no longer need to feign
any degree of cool.

I move more slowly,
take time to breathe and observe,
seek out quiet neighborhoods
where green things grow
and there is space between the houses.

There was a time when I believed that years alone
would make me wise,
but freedom came unexpectedly
under a thick cloak of invisibility;
a luxurious escape from the scrutiny
of judging eyes.

Now, I rarely walk these red-eyed streets
heavy with memories of long nights
in thin-walled apartments
where sleep was nearly impossible
due to the relentless cacophony
of other people's lives.

I lived close to the bone when I was young,
talked tough and laughed too loudly;
my friends and I congregated on street corners,
rowdy and ready for anything
except growing old.

The Scar

The scar on my leg is a jagged line
narrow at both ends, wider in the middle
resembling the webbed wings,
pointed beak, and hammer-head
of a pre-historic bird.

This spot, once a battlefield
is now as empty
as a newly conquered territory,
a monument to survival.

The scar-doctor wants to cut again,
to fold the wings inside my skin,
erase the evidence of armies
that gathered there conspiring to stage
a murderous coup.

My body's war cannot be won
even with a surgeon's knife,
this human shell will sag and wrinkle,
the eyes will lose their focus,
the bright, coarse hair turn gray.

Yet, in a place far beyond
the borders of skin and bone,
a light emerges,
a beacon of bright moon
rising above the barren skeletons
of winter trees.

From this great distance,
I look down at the scar on my leg,
that joins flesh to flesh
and wings to earth
to follow the flight
of an ancient bird
returning home.

Acknowledgements

My thanks to the editors of the following publications, in which these poems first appeared, sometimes in slightly different versions:

Evergreen Chronicles: "Strange November"

Harrington Lesbian Literary Quarterly: "Legacy" and "In the Old Neighborhood"

Lavender Review: "Distant Music," "Currents," and "Across the Table"

The Cancer Poetry Project: "First Summer"

The Queer Collection: "Descent"

The Times They Were A-Changing: Women Remember the 60s & 70s: "Under Siege" (First Place Award)

The Venomed Kiss: "Release" (as "Fitting")

Headmistress Press Books

Lovely - Lesléa Newman
Teeth & Teeth - Robin Reagler
How Distant the City - Freesia McKee
Shopgirls - Marissa Higgins
Riddle - Diane Fortney
When She Woke She Was an Open Field - Hilary Brown
God With Us - Amy Lauren
A Crown of Violets - Renée Vivien tr. Samantha Pious
Fireworks in the Graveyard - Joy Ladin
Social Dance - Carolyn Boll
The Force of Gratitude - Janice Gould
Spine - Sarah Caulfield
Diatribe from the Library - Farrell Greenwald Brenner
Blind Girl Grunt - Constance Merritt
Acid and Tender - Jen Rouse
Beautiful Machinery - Wendy DeGroat
Odd Mercy - Gail Thomas
The Great Scissor Hunt - Jessica K. Hylton
A Bracelet of Honeybees - Lynn Strongin
Whirlwind @ Lesbos - Risa Denenberg
The Body's Alphabet - Ann Tweedy
First name Barbie last name Doll - Maureen Bocka
Heaven to Me - Abe Louise Young
Sticky - Carter Steinmann
Tiger Laughs When You Push - Ruth Lehrer
Night Ringing - Laura Foley
Paper Cranes - Dinah Dietrich
On Loving a Saudi Girl - Carina Yun
The Burn Poems - Lynn Strongin
I Carry My Mother - Lesléa Newman
Distant Music - Joan Annsfire
The Awful Suicidal Swans - Flower Conroy
Joy Street - Laura Foley
Chiaroscuro Kisses - G.L. Morrison
The Lillian Trilogy - Mary Meriam
Lady of the Moon - Amy Lowell, Lillian Faderman, Mary Meriam
Irresistible Sonnets - ed. Mary Meriam
Lavender Review - ed. Mary Meriam

68274384R00027

Made in the USA
San Bernardino, CA
01 February 2018